VISUAL
MAUI

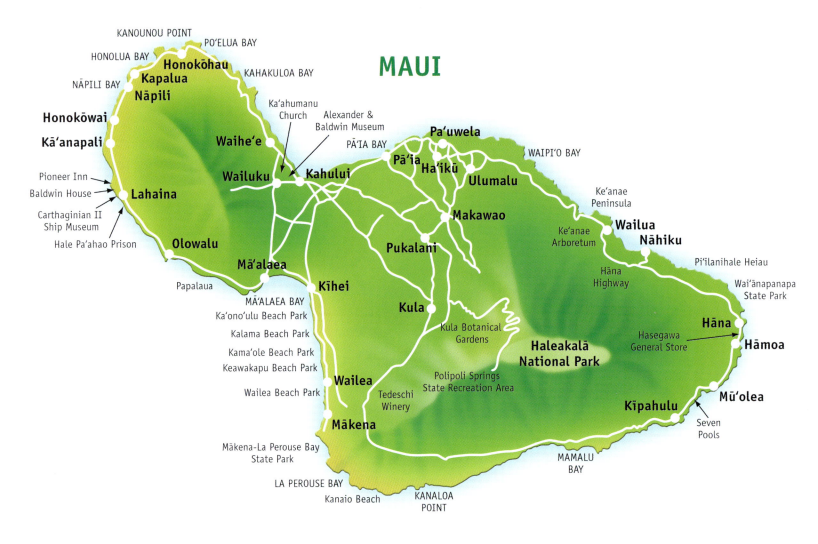

Copyright © 2005 by Mutual Publishing

No part of this book may be reproduced in any form or by any electronic or mechanical means, including information storage and retrieval devices or systems, without prior written permission from the publisher, except that brief passages may be quoted for reviews.

All rights reserved.

Design by Michael Horton Design

Library of Congress
Catalog Card Number 00-111270

ISBN 1-56647-348-9

First Printing, June 2005
1 2 3 4 5 6 7 8 9

Mutual Publishing, LLC
1215 Center Street, Suite 210
Honolulu, Hawai' 96816
Telephone (808) 732-1709
Fax (808) 734-4094
email: mutual@mutualpublishing.com
www.mutualpublishing.com

Printed in Korea

TABLE OF CONTENTS

INTRODUCTION 6

HALEAKALĀ & UPCOUNTRY 10

HĀNA & THE SOUTHEAST COAST 26

WEST MAUI 48

SOUTH MAUI 70

CENTRAL MAUI 84

INTRODUCTION

IN THE CENTER of the Hawaiian Islands—which are in the center of the Pacific Ocean and 2,500 miles away from the nearest continent—lies the enchanting island of Maui. This stunningly beautiful island is part of the most remote landmass on earth, and Maui's natural features are among the most exotic on earth. It's a staggering list: volcanoes; red-, black-, white-, and golden-sand beaches; rain forests; glorious sunrises and sunsets; and rainbows—just to name the obvious. These natural spectacles help tell the story of Maui's origin, and vivid photographic images of them are displayed in the pages that follow.

Maui is the daughter born of two separate volcanic islands which merged when then-fiery Haleakalā (East Maui) erupted ages ago and sent forth a massive wave of lava that reached the shores of a neighboring island, now West Maui. Today, a flat, seven-mile-wide isthmus connects the east and west peninsulas. It was an auspicious beginning, and the daughter of that ancient volcanic union has grown up splendidly. Indeed, Maui is blessed with the best scenery in the world and a mellow subtropical climate, but there are other

A typical, balmy day on a Maui beach complete with the shade of a palm tree and surf.

forces at work here. The island is imbued with a powerful, spiritual force—mana—that surges through her veins. It is the birthplace of Hawaiian royalty, and King Kamehameha chose Lahaina on West Maui as the first capital of the Hawaiian kingdom. These days, Maui is home to more than a hundred thousand people; and more than two million visitors a year travel from all over the world to bask in her glow.

The island was named for a legendary half-man, half-god prankster, Māui; with the help of his brothers, he fished all the Hawaiian Islands from the sea with his magical fishhook. Māui is also credited with slowing the progress of the day. His mother, the moon goddess Hina, and her friends needed more hours of sunlight to finish the chores of the day—particularly the drying of

Kanahā Beach Park *is probably the most famous windsurfing spot in Hawai‘i. On a windy day, dozens of bright sails dot the shoreline.*

The remarkable protea, *aptly named for the Greek god Proteus who could change his appearance at will, comes in a wide array of shapes and sizes. These South African transplants, like this King protea, have adapted well to the temperate climate of Kula, and have been happily adopted into island bouquets.*

kapa cloth. To accomplish this, he scampered up mighty Haleakalā and cast a great fishing net over the sun, greatly slowing its speedy retreat into night.

Perhaps Māui's feat explains why time, to this day, seems to move more slowly on Maui.

Maui is the only island in the Hawaiian archipelago named for a god. It also boasts a slew of other superlatives: Maui has the most miles of swimmable beach in Hawai'i (121 miles), and it was voted "Best Island in the World" by readers of Condé Nast Traveler magazine four years in a row. Maui's beaches are constantly ranked as some of the best in the world.

Delve into Visual Maui and you delve into the history, soul, and spectacular natural beauty of an exquisite island. You will come away with an understanding of why so many people—locals and visitors—consider that Maui nō ka 'oi: Maui is the best.

Maui is an island of contrasts. Not so far beyond the hustle and bustle of Front Street, Lahaina [bottom] are the surreal panoramas of Haleakalā [top].

HALEAKALĀ & UPCOUNTRY

EVERY DAY AT 2 A.M. alarm clocks ring all over Maui, waking visitors and a handful of residents who will make an early-morning pilgrimage up the slopes of a dormant volcano to witness the rise of the sun.

Indeed, sunrise at the summit of Haleakalā is one of the most ethereal in the world, with clouds, colors, light, and an unearthly landscape coming together to herald the birth of a fine, new day. Taking in the sunrise is an unbeatable way to start a day of exploring Haleakalā, the third-tallest volcano in Hawai'i at 10,023 feet, or the wooded trails of Polipoli, or the engaging upcountry communities of Kula, Makawao and 'Ulupalakua, which has a winery. But late-risers shouldn't be distressed. Sunset from the summit is equally spellbinding, and it's a grand way to say aloha to the day. The sun drops into the sea between neighbor islands, and the colors reflected skyward into the clouds intensify and linger long after it sets.

Haleakalā National Park *is a must-see feature of Maui. The road is narrow and curvy, but it is well-maintained and makes the summit and other park features accessible to everyone.*

The National Park Service does an outstanding job managing and explaining the 30,182-acre Haleakalā National Park. There's a $10 fee per vehicle to get in, and the pass lasts a week. It is money well spent, and the only way to get to the summit. You can hike to your heart's content, or just drive the series of overlooks and peer down into the moonish interior of the volcano that created East Maui. Plan to spend at least a day or more exploring Haleakalā and the relaxed upcountry region of Maui. You will be miles from the beaches and resorts, but you won't care.

This aerial view of the road winding up to Haleakalā National Park shows the easy, gradual slope indicative of a shield volcano, the type that created the Hawaiian Islands. Eruptions from shield volcanoes are rarely catastrophic.

[Above] **Sliding Sands Trail** *descends 2,500 feet from the Haleakalā Visitor Center parking lot to the valley floor in four miles. Most people make a quick trek to the first switchback and are rewarded with a wilderness of cinder cones and lava flow. Early Hawaiians crossed through Haleakalā via Ke'anae Valley and Kaupō Gap as secondary routes when inclement weather prohibited travel along the coast or in canoes.*

[Opposite] **Scientists from around** *the world survey the heavens from the Haleakalā Observatories.*

[Previous pages] **The crater-like** *summit of Haleakalā was not created by an explosion, but by stream erosion which carved steep, massive valleys into the volcanic mountain. Subsequent lava flows filled in these valleys, giving the impression of a rim.*

The dawn of a new day emerges across a vivid plateau of cloud banks and mountain peaks at Haleakalā, the volcano that formed East Maui. More than a million people a year visit the summit of 10,023-foot Haleakalā to observe its mysterious grandeur. Now classified as a dormant volcano, Haleakalā was born approximately 1.7 million years ago. The last eruption occurred around 1790 near Mākena. Scientists believe the sleeping giant could erupt again.

17 HALEAKALĀ & UPCOUNTRY

[Above] **The nēnē goose** is the Hawai'i state bird. It is endangered, but about two-hundred find sanctuary within Haleakalā National Park. Park staff urge people not to feed nēnē. They will sometimes approach vehicles and roadways looking for handouts, often with tragic consequences.

The desolate interior of Haleakalā has been compared to the surface of the moon.

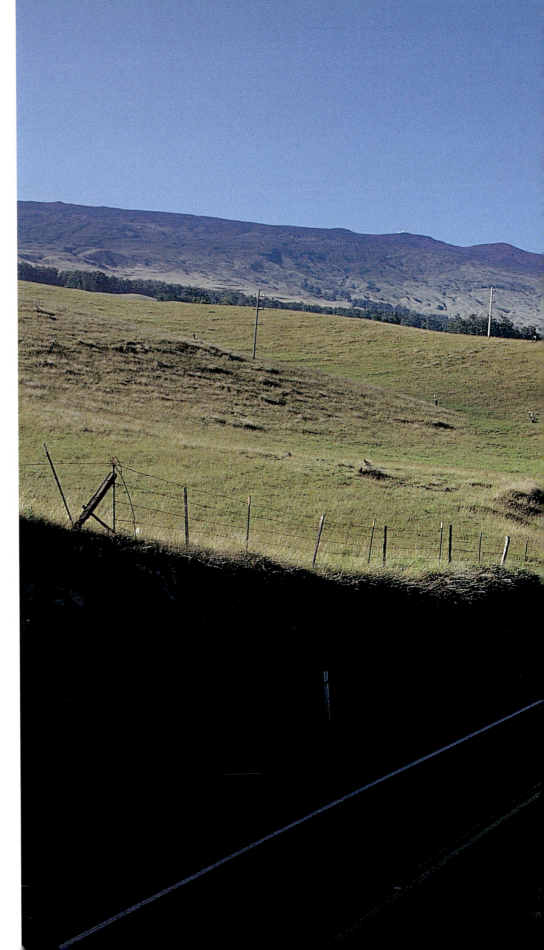

HALEAKALĀ & UPCOUNTRY

The rolling meadows *and pasture lands of Upcountry Maui exemplify Maui's rustic side.*

[Above] **Hawaiians call the** endemic silversword plant 'āhinahina. The silvery gray "hairs" on its leaves are a remarkable adaptation to the harsh, high-elevation environment because of their ability to conserve moisture and reflect the sun's rays.

[Opposite] **The geometrical waves** of growing crops grace the slopes of Haleakalā.

The crumbly red sand at Kaihalulu Beach on Haleakalā's east-facing shore is actually eroded lava cinders from neighboring Ka'uiki Head cinder cone. The lava at this site contains a high amount of iron, which oxidizes when exposed to air and results in the unusual rust-colored sand.

HĀNA & THE SOUTHEAST COAST

VISITING MAUI WOULD be incomplete without exploring the Hāna District's north and south coasts. The North coast is Maui's lushest coastline, stretching from Keʻanae in the north to Kaupō in the south. Mentally, Hāna begins as soon as you pass Hoʻokipa, where ocean, mountain and stream come together. You can sense the jungle, and soon the road leads there.

And so begins an odyssey which can take two hours or more one-way, with endless curves and one-lane bridges, and sometimes, a line of vehicles ahead of and behind you. Relief is close at hand, though. A series of roadside waterfalls invite road-weary bodies, and fruit stands abound with inexpensive bananas, papayas, avocados and other delicacies of the island.

On the breathtaking Keʻanae Peninsula, taro, a prime staple of the Hawaiian diet, is cultivated in great, sodden patches of land. Down the road are the legendary Waiʻānapanapa sea caves and a fabulous black-sand beach. Nearby is Hawaiʻi's largest and oldest heiau, an ancient site of worship, built around the 15th-century. Every turn of the road inspires more questions, more exploration.

[Above] **A brand-new** day dawns on the north coast of the Hāna District.

[Opposite] **Waimoku Falls in** the Kīpahulu District plunges straight down a sheer rock amphitheater. Sunlight plays upon the cascading water, often enlightening the area with dozens of small rainbows. The falls are accessible by crossing the road out of the parking lot at Kīpahulu and hiking uphill along a marked trail.

The road continues to the picturesque village of Hāna, to Kīpahulu's Pools of ʻOheʻo, which tumble spectacularly from mountain to ocean. Proceed, and the jungle turns abruptly into the arid ranch land of Kaupō. With all the changes there is one constant. Massive Haleakalā seems to stand watch over the entire journey like a silent sentinel.

Manawainui Falls can be seen from the large concrete bridge that spans the lower part of Manawainui Stream between Kīpahulu and Kaupō. Although the area receives a lot of rain, the ground here is so porous that the stream is often dry.

Taro is a culturally and nutritionally important tuberous root used by Hawaiians to make poi. It requires lots of hard, physical labor and large patches of land soaked in fresh water. The Ke'anae Peninsula is famous for its large taro fields, or lo'i.

Over the millennia, *the ocean and wind have carved dramatic sea arches and sheer cliffs out of the Keʻanae Peninsula. A dramatic way to view the mesmerizing northern Hāna coastline is to fly over it.*

[Above] **Those who visit** 'Ohe'o Gulch seldom venture to the upper pools. Those who do are rewarded with a well-maintained trail that leads uphill through a dense bamboo forest and culminates at Waimoku Falls, a waterfall that plunges straight down a pali so steep you have to crane your neck all the way back to take it in. Waimoku Falls splashes into a shallow, rocky pool at the bottom perfect for soaking tired feet.

[Opposite] **Wai'ānapanapa's famous black**-sand beach is a compelling place to ponder the geological history of the Hawaiian Islands, or just about anything. The beach is part of Wai'ānapanapa State Park, which is open to campers with tents and trailers and to those who obtain one of several cabins available through early reservations.

[Above] **Expert weavers display** baskets woven from coconut-palm leaves along the Hāna Highway.

[Opposite] **Relying on a** sense of honor among passersby, many Hāna residents offer the fruits of their gardens for a minimal price at roadside fruit and flower stands.

HĀNA

The striking black- sand beach at Wai'ānapanapa State Park is a must-stop destination. A well-marked trail leads to a sea cave where, according to legend, a Hawaiian princess was slain by her jealous husband. An ancient path hugs the coast, making for a nice walk. Offshore, the snorkeling is good on calm days, but beware of a steep drop-off.

[Following pages] **Described by author** James Michener as the quintessential tropical beach, Hāmoa Bay glistens invitingly as it laps against the sandy beach maintained by the Hotel Hāna-Maui.

Cascading sheaths of water, like this one along Hāna Highway, dot the windward coastlines and cliffsides of most Hawaiian Islands.

To get to *Hāna, most people brave the winding, 52-mile-long Hāna Highway, with its 600 or so curves and 54 one-lane bridges. Those who arrive by plane save time, but miss out on spectacular roadside scenery like waterfalls, dramatic vistas around every turn, groves of fragrant wild ginger, fruit-laden trees, and much more.*

A cascade of *cool mountain water falls and spills over itself down the slopes of Haleakalā into the turbulent waves of the Pacific Ocean below. In its wake, an enticing chain of fresh-water pools attract many to the Kīpahulu District, the other side of Haleakalā National Park. Dozens of tourists and locals come here to swim in the pools, but they are often deserted in the late afternoon and early morning.*

WEST MAUI

WEST MAUI WAS ONCE its own island, and in many ways it still is. It has its own mountain range, miles of sunny beaches, splashy resorts, plus a rich and compelling history.

Indeed, West Maui seems to have it all, and the ancient Hawaiians were the first to discover the relative ease of life along its protected leeward shore. Beginning at the foot of the pali north of Māʻalaea, a string of roadside beaches tempt drivers all the way to Lahaina.

Lahaina Harbor is a prime vantage point for watching sunsets and for strolling among the boats berthed in its small harbor.

Great whaling ships began making Lahaina a regular anchorage in 1819, and Protestant missionaries from New England were close on their heels. Successful in converting Hawaiians to Christianity, the pious missionaries had more trouble restoring moral order among the rowdy seamen. Today, Lahaina reigns as Maui's most energetic town, as a stroll down Front Street will prove.

The Pioneer Mill began cultivating sugar in 1862. Until recently, sugarcane flourished from Olowalu to Honokōwai. In 1961, the Kāʻanapali Beach resort opened and over the next few decades West Maui transformed again as tourism became the economic base.

North of Kāʻanapali is the ritzy resort area of Kapalua and dramatic, windswept beaches. West Maui becomes more peaceful past Kapalua, with far less development and fewer cars on the road. Uninterrupted views of pineapple fields, the Pacific Ocean and Molokaʻi are in one direction. On the other side the unmolested peaks of the West Maui Mountains gather rain to nourish the quiet villages in valleys below.

Eventually the road runs into the isthmus separating East and West Maui. Haleakalā is in view, a perfect opportunity to note the differences between two islands that form one.

[Right] **Jagged peaks and** *deep, mysterious valleys typify the West Maui Mountains near Olowalu.*

[Previous page] **Miles of sun**-*soaked coastline make West Maui one of the world's most coveted playgrounds. The vivid hues of sunset last many long minutes after the sun sinks behind the island of Lāna'i.*

[Left] **The West Maui** Mountains rank as one of the most rugged mountain ranges in Hawai'i. Vertical cliffs, razor-backed ridges, and deep valleys help keep much of the range inaccessible.

The tallest peak of the West Maui Mountains is Pu'u Kukui, standing at 5,788 feet. It is one of the wettest spots in the world, receiving approximately 40 feet of rain annually. Lahaina town, which is only seven miles away, stands in the shadow of the mountains and, interestingly, receives only a few inches of rain a year.

[Following pages] **The first of** the wild and woolly whale hunters arrived in Lahaina in 1819, and the town was never the same. Drunken sailors roamed the town arm-in-arm with native girls who swam out to the ships to greet them. Christian missionaries from New England weren't far behind, invited by Queen Keōpūolani, the highest ranking of Kamehameha's twenty or so wives. The war between sailor and missionary raged for decades until the whaling industry died a slow death.

[Above] **The restored Lahaina-**Kāʻanapali and Pacific Railroad, aka the sugarcane train, chugs along the tracks between Lahaina and Kāʻanapali through sugarcane fields. The train is pulled by an 1890s-vintage steam locomotive which harkens back to the old sugar plantation days.

[Above] **The landmark Pioneer Inn**, *built in 1901 to accommodate interisland passengers, is still a popular grog shop and lodge for travelers who want to stay in the heart of Lahaina town. Errol Flynn was a famous guest, and Spencer Tracy stayed here during filming of the movie* Devil at Four O'Clock. *The top floor has rooms; the bar and various shops and sundry stores are on the bottom floor.*

The view of *historic Lahaina from the anchorage in front of town has changed since the days when as many as 400 whaling ships moored here at one time. Front Street is lined with shops, bars, restaurants, and art galleries.*

[Above] **The Kā‘anapali Resort** opened in 1961 as Hawai‘i's first master-planned resort. Golden-sand beaches, first-class accommodations and incredible views of the Pacific Ocean, neighbor islands and the West Maui Mountains make Kā‘anapali an ideal destination for vacationers.

[Opposite] **The Wo Hing** Temple, a former religious site and meeting hall for the Chinese in Lahaina, now operates as a museum on Front Street. The Wo Hing Society, which built the temple in 1909 to maintain social and political ties with their homeland, still exists.

Fanned by gentle trade winds, and perfectly positioned for viewing the West Maui Mountains, Moloka'i, and Lāna'i, Kā'anapali Beach on Maui's west shore is one of the finest beaches in the world. Average temperatures on Maui range from 75 to 85 degrees Fahrenheit, making for perfect beach weather almost every day.

[Above] **Sunlight gives way** *to dusk as torches light up beachfront Kāʻanapali.*

[Opposite] **Handsome Cook pine** *trees line this street in Kapalua. Every square inch of the Kapalua resort area reflects an aesthetic zeal.*

[Following pages] **An audience of** *palm trees seems to lean toward the horizon to absorb the final moments of daylight.*

Fleming Beach Park *is the northernmost jewel in a string of large, sandy beaches along Maui's west-facing shoreline. Bathed by refreshing trade winds and ample shade trees, it is an inviting place to splash in the surf and watch honu, green sea turtles, come up for air close to shore. This lovely beach can be unpredictable, however, with high surf and a strong riptide possible during winter months.*

SOUTH MAUI

STARTING AT MĀʻALAEA and ending at La Pérouse Bay, South Maui has the island's most consistently sunny coastline. The numerous white-sand beaches of Māʻalaea, Kīhei, Wailea, and Mākena are shielded from rain by towering Haleakalā.

The reliable weather makes taking a snorkel trip from Māʻalaea Harbor to Molokini Marine Life Conservation District, a tiny, crescent-shaped islet about three miles off the South Maui coast, a splendid way to spend half a day. The surrounding waters are full of marine life.

The sandy shores and wetlands hugging Māʻalaea Bay are vital habitat for a number of endangered creatures. In the sand dunes off Highway 31, female hawksbill sea turtles come ashore to lay eggs. Neighboring Keālia Pond National Wildlife Refuge is a critical nesting area for endemic waterbirds like the aeʻo and the ʻalae keʻokeʻo. Offshore, a huge swath of ocean comprises the Hawaiian Islands Humpback Whale National Marine Sanctuary.

Moonlit tranquility from *a Wailea Beach.*

Although the town of Kīhei is a crowded, unplanned maze of concrete and high-rises, its beautiful beaches provide refuge from the congested town, and accommodations here are less expensive than at Kāʻanapali and Wailea.

Wailea, just south of Kīhei, has been groomed into a world class resort featuring luxury hotels, a swank shopping and dining center, and access to fantastic beaches. The paved road ends in Mākena, where the landscape runs wilder, and open space and several undeveloped beaches prevail.

The first European to set foot on Maui was not Captain Cook, but French explorer Jean-Francois de Galaup, Comte de La Pérouse, who, in 1786, anchored in the protected bay south of Mākena which was named for him. Ruins from an ancient Hawaiian village lies beyond the bay, and a footpath heads east toward Hāna.

Seekers of history, sun-soaked beaches, and a slew of ocean recreational activities will enjoy South Maui.

[Above] **All types of** boating trips can be arranged from South Maui, most originating out of Māʻalaea Harbor. Snorkel and sailing excursions are especially popular, and whale-watching off South Maui is excellent from December through May. The island of Lānaʻi, a popular snorkeling destination, beckons in the distance.

The protected water *of Mōkapu Beach is one of Wailea's choice swimming spots. Snorkeling off the rocky outcrop and along the first reef just offshore is usually very good. A palm tree provides a patch of midday shade.*

"**The coco-palm** groves of the Pacific have a strangeness and witchery of their own. As I write now I hear the moaning rustle of the wind through their plume-like tops, and their long slender stems, and crisp crown of leaves above the trees…"

—British traveler and writer Isabella Bird,
Six Months in the Sandwich Islands, *1875*

[Above] **The Renaissance Wailea** *Beach Resort is located on Mōkapu Beach, one of Maui's most beautiful waterfronts. Viewed from this vantage point, West Maui in the distance appears to be its own island.*

[Opposite] **Divers and snorkelers** *flock to Molokini Islet aboard charter boats to observe an amazing diversity of sea life. The whole area is protected as a Marine Life Conservation District, and species like giant manta rays and whale sharks, plus hundreds of other sea creatures, can be spotted here.*

The placid, turquoise water off Mākena's Big Beach belies the fact that it is the third most dangerous beach in Hawai'i, due to its powerful, neck-snapping shorebreak. Sandy Beach on O'ahu and Kā'anapali Beach in West Maui rank as the first and second, respectively. Getting slammed into the sand or reef by a huge wave is no fun, so know your limits.

'Āhihi-Kīna'u Natural Area
Reserve south of Mākena is one of Maui's best and most popular snorkel sites. The long lava finger in the background is Cape Kīna'u, part of the last lava flow to surge out of Haleakalā around 1790.

The first Europeans to set foot on Maui's shores arrived in 1786 with the two-ship fleet commanded by French navigator Jean François de La Pérouse. Pérouse and his crew sailed by Kīpahulu, Kaupō and the Kanaio coasts, but could not find suitable anchorage until they reached Maui's southernmost bay, known then by Hawaiians as Keoneʻōʻio. Eventually the bay was renamed for La Pérouse. An ancient footpath leads from the bay to Kaupō.

CENTRAL MAUI

MOST PEOPLE LAND AT Kahului Airport and cruise right through Central Maui on their way to the resorts of South and West Maui without giving the area much thought. Those who return to explore Central Maui a little further are rewarded with an area rich in history, culture, and diversion. Museums, theaters, practical shopping and dining opportunities, hiking, and several noteworthy sites make a day spent in Central Maui worthwhile.

Central Maui is where the people live. Approximately a third of Maui's 120,000 or so people reside in Kahului and Wailuku. Kahului has the main airport, a community college and a thriving commercial base. Wailuku serves as the county seat for all of Maui County, including the islands of Lāna'i and Moloka'i.

Wailuku was also a political stronghold for the Hawaiian monarchy. Its name means "waters of destruction" and in 1790 a brutal, decisive battle between the armies of Big Island chief Kamehameha the First and Maui's chief Kalanikupule raged at 'Īao Stream. 'Īao Valley, famous today for the 1,200-foot 'Īao Needle, was also a sacred burial ground for revered Hawaiian chiefs.

When Protestant missionaries from New England arrived on Maui in 1823, life was irrevocably changed for the Hawaiians. The Bailey House Museum, on the way to 'Īao Valley, is a fine place to learn more about both cultures.

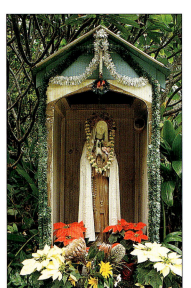

A sign of quiet refuge- outside 'Īao Valley.

Maui's sugar industry was born in Wailuku. By 1860, sugar growing was an active agricultural industry on Maui, and the valuable crop was shipped from the various ports on Maui. Miles of irrigation ditches were later dug into the mountains, and the dry, low-lying isthmus between East and West Maui grew green with sugarcane fields.

Sugarcane is being phased out of island economics, but the towns of Wailuku and Kahului, and the rest of Central Maui, are rolling with the changes.

[Above] **ʻĪao Valley is** the site of a fierce, historic battle between the armies of Big Island chief Kamehameha the First and Maui chief Kalanikupule near the end of the eighteenth century. Kamehameha and his warriors slaughtered the Maui forces with slingshots, spears, pure force, and cannons borrowed from foreign, or haole, sympathizers. The Maui chief fled on a hidden footpath that leads from ʻĪao Valley to Olowalu on Maui's west side, then sailed to Oʻahu, leaving his warriors behind to fight hopelessly against Kamehameha's superior strength. It is reported that ʻĪao Stream became so clogged with corpses that the stream surged backwards and its water ran red with blood.

[Right] **Razor-backed peaks,** sheer cliffs and dense vegetation make the interior of ʻĪao Valley almost impenetrable.

[Previous page] **ʻĪao Needle points** toward the heavens at ʻĪao Valley State Park. The 1,200-foot stone pillar is actually a tough, basaltic rock core that was carved by eons of stream erosion. ʻĪao means supreme cloud or supreme light in Hawaiian

Heritage Gardens, at 'Īao Valley's Kepaniwai Park, was built for all of Hawai'i's people. Architect Richard Tongg included a thatched-roof Hawaiian grass shack, a Japanese teahouse and garden, a Portuguese villa, a Chinese pagoda, a New England "salt box" and a bamboo house. It's hard to imagine that this serene spot was the site of one of Hawai'i's most brutal massacres. Near the end of the eighteenth century, a Big Island army, led by chief Kamehameha the First, annihilated Maui soldiers in a historic, infamous battle.

The Bailey House Museum serves as a monument to two cultures: the Hawaiian and the missionary. Built of stone, mortar, and wood, the house was built from 1833 to 1850. In the 1840s it was the Wailuku Female Seminary, a boarding school for young women who were groomed to become good Christian wives for the young men attending Lahainaluna School in Lahaina. Edward Bailey, who served as principal for the girls' school and later as manager for the Wailuku Sugar Company, lived here with his wife Caroline for more than half a century.

The Hawaiian Room displays excellent, authentic examples of pre-contact tools and artifacts, including kapa cloth, woven lauhala mats, and a large wood carving of the pig god Kamapuaʻa. The sacred image is one of few that survived when the ancient Hawaiian religious system collapsed after the arrival of Protestant missionaries.

Windsurfing is a *popular sport and the waves at Ho'okipa Beach Park provide the perfect adrenaline rush for those out to conquer the rushing waves and winds.*

Ka'ahumanu Congregational Church is a Wailuku landmark. Built in 1876, the Protestant church was named for Hāna-born Queen Ka'ahumanu. The queen was an important early convert to Christianity and a favorite wife of King Kamehameha. On Sundays, the congregation sings hymns and prays in Hawaiian.

Built in 1897 *by Portuguese laborers, the octagonal building of the Holy Ghost Hall of Our Lady Queen of Angels Church stands alone past the small town of Kula.*

A quiet moment *is captured during moonset from Kahului Harbor. The harbor is the only deep-draft commercial port serving the island.*

Although the Hāna District begins geographically at the Keʻanae Peninsula and ends at Kaupō, it seems to start on the open road just past the famed windsurfing mecca at Hoʻokipa Beach Park, pictured here.

[Above] **Vanda orchids reach** *for the sun on the central isthmus separating East and West Maui.*

[Opposite] **One of Hawai'i's** *last natural ponds, necessary habitat for native Hawaiian waterfowl, Keālia Pond National Wildlife Refuge provides sanctuary for these ae'o, or Hawaiian stilts, and other animals. Endangered hawksbill sea turtles come to the beach and sand dunes of the refuge to lay their eggs from July to December. Other native life found here are the Hawaiian duck or koloa maoli, the Hawaiian coot ('alae ke'oke'o) and the 'auku'u, or black-crowned night heron. The 400-acre refuge is nestled between Mā'alaea Bay and the sugarcane fields of north Kīhei.*

Scenes like this one of Central Maui cane fields will someday be a vision of the past. Sugarcane, which requires one ton of water to make merely a pound of sugar, is no longer cost-effective to grow in Hawai'i and many plantations, including Pioneer Mill in Lahaina, have been forced to shut down.

Mā'alaea Bay, as *seen from the lookout at McGregor Point, is part of the Hawaiian Islands Humpback Whale National Marine Sanctuary, and is a favorite "nursery" among mother humpback whales who migrate from Arctic waters every winter to breed and give birth in Hawaiian waters. The nearly cloudless summit of Haleakalā can be seen in the distance.*

Watching the sun *set while suspended in a hammock anywhere on Maui is highly recommended.*